For what age group is this book?

This book is for adults and young adults because it explains mature concepts about progressing happily in life. Simple examples are used to make it easier for parents and teachers to educate children of different age groups about this complex subject. High school students can read the book on their own and reflect upon the thoughts presented here or discuss the ideas with their peers, teachers, or parents.

Chapters

Awareness Books for Children
P.O. Box 2495
Edmond, Oklahoma 73083-2495

Website: awarenessbooksforchildren.org

My special thanks to:

My husband Vivek and
my children Uday & Supriya

Randy Anderson

Ralonda Wood

Kristi Kenney

Sherry Vowel

Nikita Kohli

Family & Friends

This book is dedicated to my children. Some of their words have made an everlasting impression on my mind:

"Mom, these are not your limitations, they are your hurdles; you can cross them."

"Mom, you will do well. Even if you make a mistake, you are one of those who can laugh at their mistakes."

Like all parents, I, too, learn from my children!

A note to all my readers

We all strive to be happy and successful in life. Although lasting happiness is related to progressing in life by building relationships and by being content, many of us associate our happiness or success with having more money, power, popularity, or awards. This book presents powerful ideas on succeeding in life in a straightforward and unique manner, connecting several topics in psychology such as happiness, self-esteem, mindfulness, social and emotional learning, motivation, fear, courage, grit, resilience, relationship building, and Maslow's hierarchy of needs. Because there is a lot of information, read this book slowly, meditate upon the thoughts presented here, and correlate your personal experiences to the ideas expressed in this book; pondering on these concepts can help develop a thorough understanding of progressing happily in life. It is then important to apply these thoughts in your day-to-day lives.

A note to parents, teachers, and guardians

Adults play a significant role in helping children develop self-esteem and healthy habits. Several examples in this book can apply to younger students; the purpose of these simple examples is to make it easier for parents, teachers, and guardians to educate children of different age groups about this complex subject.

Reinforcing the message is important. Adults can tailor their approach according to the age of the children; they are encouraged to be innovative by converting the statements in this book into questions, utilizing additional resources, engaging in various activities, and sharing personal stories and experiences.

I hope that this book can help make a difference.

Best wishes,

Neeti Kohli, M.D.

CHAPTER 1 – UNDERSTANDING DESIRES, FEARS, AND COURAGE

The statement "I can face my fears to follow my dreams" has two components:

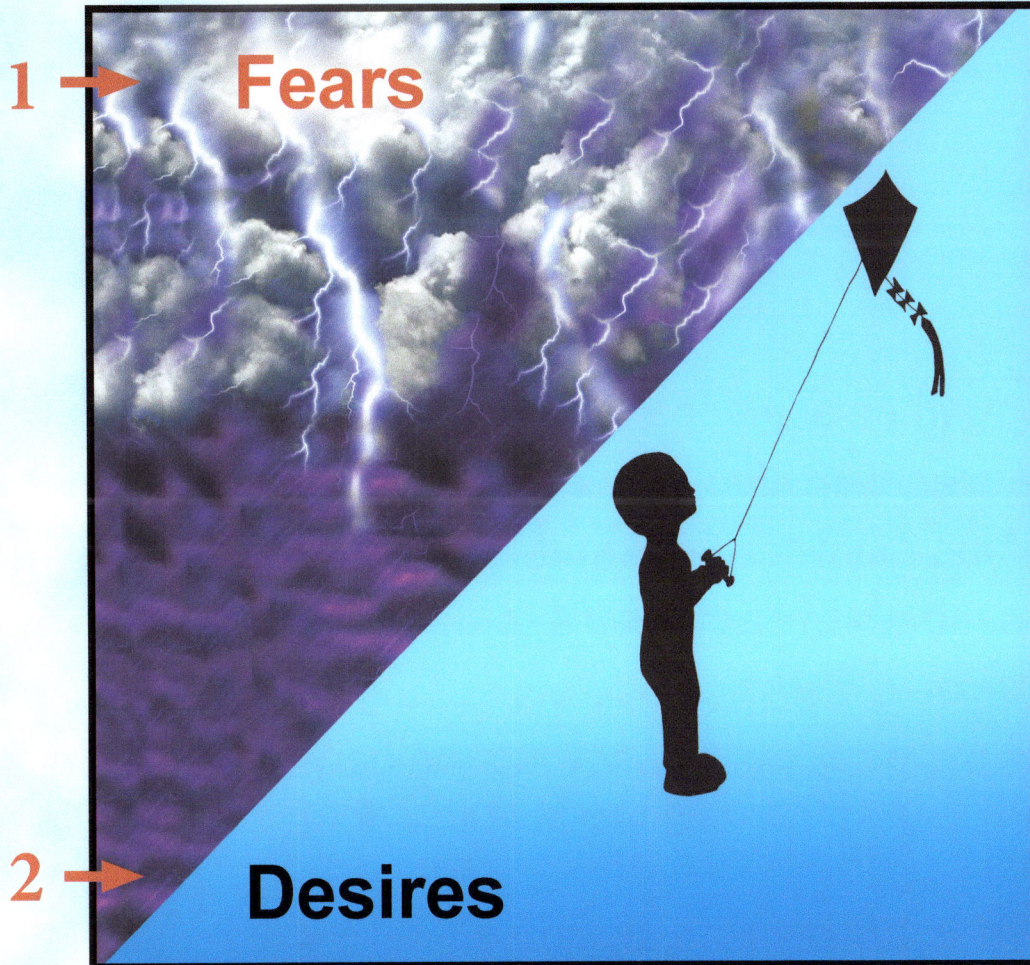

1 → **Fears**

2 → **Desires**

Both fears and desires come from the needs that we all have. Therefore, to understand our fears and desires, we should first understand our needs.

We all have the same needs.
Fulfilling our needs makes us happy.

WHAT DO I NEED?

I need food, water, clothes, and shelter; I need money to buy these basic necessities.

I need to bond with others and build relationships.

I feel happy when someone …

- Understands my feelings, my thoughts, and me.

- Comforts me when I am hurt.

- Helps me when I am unable to do something on my own.

- Appreciates me when I do something good.

- Helps me progress by showing me how to correct my mistakes or by guiding me to improve my skills and talents.

- Listens to my opinions because I have different knowledge, experiences, and perspectives.

- Joins me for fun activities.

- Works with me for the betterment of society.

I need to progress in life.

I feel happy when I progress.

I have three roles in life: I am an individual, a member of various groups, and a part of society. Therefore, there are many ways by which I can progress. My progress is about …

A. Self-improvement, which means I improve my relationships, habits, talents, abilities, and knowledge.

B. Advancement of my family and the groups with whom I work.

C. Betterment of society, in which I contribute to improving issues affecting our society. Because I am a part of society, improvement of society is also my progress.

I need to protect myself physically, emotionally, and socially.

I feel happy when I stay healthy and I am treated with equality and respect. Therefore, preventing injuries and preserving my self-esteem is important.

Desires are <u>thoughts</u> about fulfilling our needs.

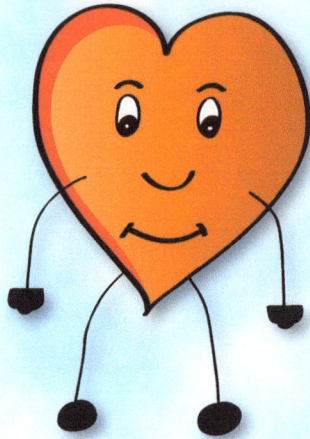

A need for food, clothes, and shelter
"I desire to have enough money for my needs."

A need to bond
"I desire to have trustworthy friends."

A need to progress
"I desire to improve my skills."

A need to protect
"I desire to stand against and stop the person who is bullying me."

Fears are <u>thoughts</u> about <u>not</u> being able to fulfill our needs.

1. Not fulfilling the need for food, water, clothes, and shelter

    "My dad lost his job. I fear that my family will not have food and a place to live."

2. Not fulfilling the need to bond with others

    "I fear being lonely."

    "I fear I will have an argument."

    "I fear my friends will laugh at me and not accept me in the group."

3. Not fulfilling the need to progress in life

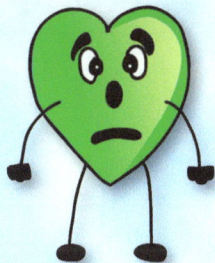

"I fear I will fail my test."

"I fear I will lose the competition."

"I fear I will forget on stage."

"I fear I will not get the result I expect."

"I fear failure."

4. Not fulfilling the need to protect ourselves

"I fear I will get injured."

"I fear someone will bully me and hurt me emotionally."

"I fear I will not be treated with equality and respect by society."

Asking ourselves the question "What are my fears?" helps us develop the understanding of the risks involved in taking a particular action.

What are the risks involved if I take a particular action?

Will someone laugh at my mistake?
Will I fail?
Will I get injured?
Will I be punished?
What else might happen?

Fear = Understanding Risks

When we understand the risks associated with our actions, we either inhibit ourselves from taking action or get energized to take action. Both choices can have beneficial and harmful effects.

With fear, we inhibit ourselves and stop taking action.

1. Beneficial Effect

With fear, we become careful; we think of risks first, and then we inhibit ourselves.

"I will not jump from the roof. That would be stupid."

"I will never text while driving. I fear I will hurt myself or others."

"I can be punished if I plagiarize to get an award. I am not going to cheat."

2. Harmful Effects

A. With fear, we inhibit ourselves so much that it prevents us from progressing in our lives or building honest relationships.

"I fear getting poor grades. I am so anxious that I cannot focus on studying."

"Acting is my passion, but I fear that people will laugh at me; therefore, I don't try."

"I fear telling the truth will result in an argument, so I hide the facts."

B. With fear, we wrongly inhibit ourselves from standing for honesty, equality, and respect.

"I saw my friend plagiarizing; however, I said nothing because it could hurt our friendship."

"I saw one student bullying another student at school. I didn't tell him to stop or report it because he could hurt me too.

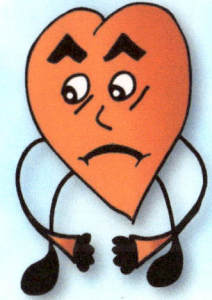

With fear, we get energized to take action.

1. Beneficial Effect

With fear, we can become courageous. We understand the risks, get encouraged to make a plan, and work hard to overcome those risks.

"I fear I will get poor grades; therefore, I am going to work hard and try my best."

"I fear someone will laugh at my singing; therefore, I am going to practice and get better."

2. Harmful Effects

With fear, we may begin to lie, hate, cheat, or retaliate.

"I fear telling the truth will cause an argument; therefore, I lie."

"I fear I will not pass the test; therefore, I will cheat."

"I fear she will hurt me. I hate her, and I am going to hurt her."

Fear has a positive role.

The primary functions of fear are to …

- Inhibit us to protect ourselves.

- Motivate us to think of methods to overcome risks.

Fear protects me every day. It helps me to be careful and prevents me from doing something reckless. For example, I cross the road carefully because I fear getting hurt.

Fear helps me understand my risks. Then, I can plan and become courageous to face my fears.

However, if we let fear inhibit us and keep us from following our dreams with integrity, or let fear make us lie, cheat, hate, or retaliate, then we change its positive role into negative. Thus, we see the harmful effects of fear. Sometimes, fear is not even real. It is a false perception. Our false perception can harm us or others.

I was angry at my friend for ignoring me. Later, I realized that it was a simple misunderstanding.

Fear has a positive role when we embrace it: we utilize our concerns to challenge ourselves and plan our journey to progress in our lives. We should accept that there are some risks involved in every action we take and not let those risks inhibit us from advancing in life with integrity. We should be courageous.

Courage is taking thoughtful actions after understanding the risks. It requires knowledge, planning, hard work, and the strength to accept adverse outcomes if they happen.

We need courage to

Protect everyone's rights and stand up for equality and respect:

- **We fight against our temptations to lie, cheat, hate, or hurt others.**

"It is tempting, but I will not criticize others to make myself more popular."

- **We stand against people who are treating others with disrespect.**

"I will stand up against people who are bullying others."

Improve ourselves and our relationships:

- **We overcome our fear of not progressing.**

"I fear that I will not get selected in the audition, but I am going to work very hard, practice, and try."

- **We overcome our fear of not building relationships.**

"I fear that I am going to have an argument that may damage my relationship, but I will communicate calmly, openly, and honestly."

We feel happy when we are courageous and challenge ourselves to progress in life or to stand for equality and respect.

The word fear has two implications: emotion and thought.

Generally, we see fear as an emotion that is experienced when there is an imminent threat of bodily or emotional injury. However, in this book the word fear is presented as a thought. Fearful thoughts can result in different emotions like anxiety, anger, caution, or motivation; fearful thoughts can lead to wrong actions or careful actions. The choice is ours: we can make fearful thoughts have a negative or positive role.

CHAPTER 2 – PROGRESSING IN LIFE

To progress in life is a need that we all have. This is an ongoing process that never stops. Even if we progress a lot on one day, we still need to keep improving on the following days. Just as we eat a large meal on one day, we still need to eat on the following days.

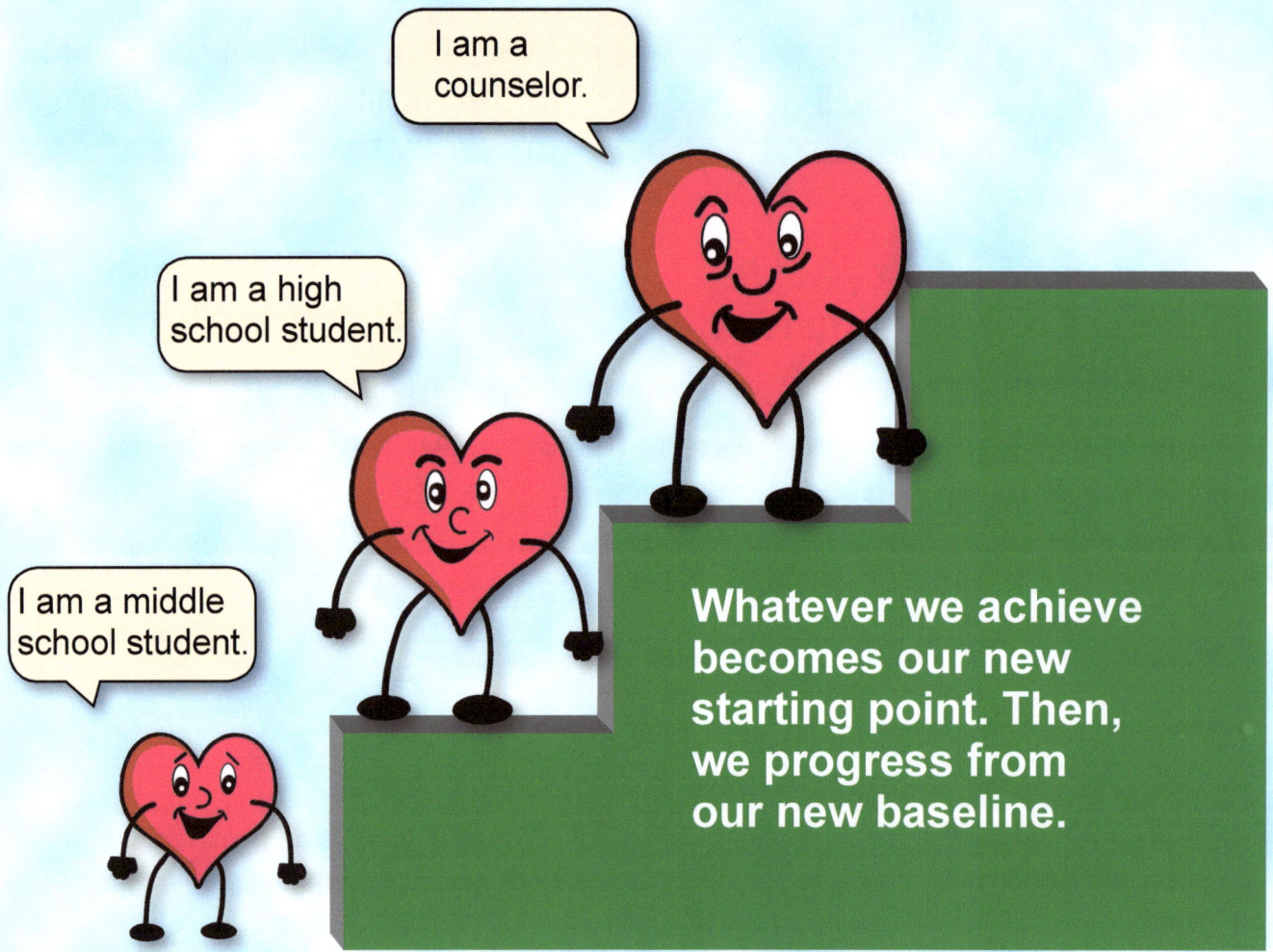

I am a counselor.

I am a high school student.

I am a middle school student.

Whatever we achieve becomes our new starting point. Then, we progress from our new baseline.

Our progress is about …

1. Self-improvement.

2. Advancement of our family and the groups with whom we work.

3. Betterment of society.

Progressing in life makes us happy. Money, power, popularity, grades, and awards are indicators that help us measure or see our progress; that is why they make us happy when we obtain them. They are good if we get them by working hard and by being honest on our journey to pursue our dreams. They are bad if we make them primary goals and begin to hurt others or ourselves.

I have been practicing piano every day since I was in fifth grade. Now people love to hear me play. I am popular at my school.

I have to win the competition. I am going to cheat.

If we make money, power, importance, or awards our primary goals, we begin to link our failures and successes to these aims. We can misinterpret our progress as a failure.

I was expecting to win the competition, but I lost. Why did this happen to me? I worked so hard. I am a real loser. I am going to quit.

The choice is ours: we can have a negative or a positive approach when the outcome is different from our expectations.

I didn't win the competition even though I worked very hard. I may lose a competition, but I am not a loser. I may fail a test, but I am not a failure. I understand that I will not get the result that I expect all the time. Therefore, I do not consider myself a failure. I am successful because I have improved and I will continue to progress with hard work and integrity.

True success in life is an ongoing progress. Even if we do not get the result that we expect each time, we are still successful because we have improved and progressed.

Failure is not about losing; it is about giving up or not making an effort.

Money, awards, power, and importance can also tempt us to hurt others by cheating, lying, or discriminating. By doing so, we may get better measurable results, but we lose our integrity and we lose our happiness.

I WANTED TO WIN. Therefore, I stole my competitor's computer. She couldn't submit her project, and I got the award. I am now the winner.

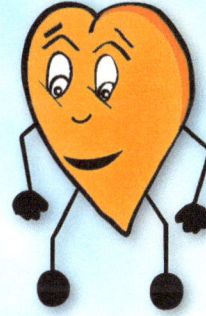

Money, power, popularity, or awards should not be our passions. They are the results of our passions. Real happiness lies in challenging ourselves for self-improvement and for the betterment of society.

If we obtain money, power, popularity, or awards easily, without working hard, we may feel that we have succeeded; however, in reality, we have not progressed. Getting rewards without putting in effort is a fake success that takes away our ability to challenge ourselves.

I can easily run three miles. Even though I was walking in a one-mile race, I got a huge trophy for participation. My family and I are very happy because I got a giant trophy.

To progress in life is a need, but if we do not set goals and work hard to progress, then we may look for ways to make us feel that we are progressing. We may begin to gossip, criticize others, and laugh at others' mistakes; we may even start bullying and begin to belittle them.

He is stupid. He doesn't even know how to do simple math.

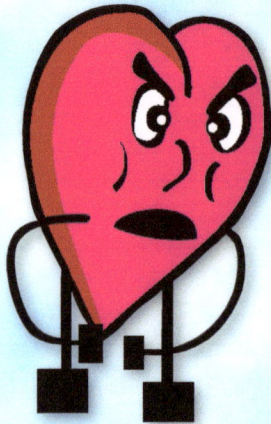

She has a funny voice. I laugh every time she speaks.

We take these incorrect steps if we are envious of others or because of our insecurities or lack of progress. These behaviors give us a false feeling of being powerful and successful, but they bring unhappiness into our lives.

Our goal should be to progress in life by building relationships and helping each other improve.

CHAPTER 3 – BALANCING THOUGHTS AND UNDERSTANDING CONTENTMENT

We are all on a journey to progress in life. We set goals and then work hard to follow our dreams. Pursuing our dreams is like an airplane flying to reach a new destination.

Before an airplane takes off, it balances its weight for a smooth and comfortable ride. Similarly, before we begin our quest to follow our dreams, it is important that we balance our thoughts for a happy, enjoyable journey.

Just like an airplane, there are two wings to **balanced thoughts**:

Wing One

Respecting Ourselves

Respecting Others

Wing Two

Positive thoughts about ourselves

Positive thoughts about others

Our **thoughts are unbalanced** when …

We think poorly about ourselves.

We have low self-esteem and feel worthless. We are not happy with ourselves.

or

We think poorly about others.

We are egotistic and begin to hurt others. We feel that we are better than others in every way.

Unbalanced Thoughts

Low Self-Esteem

The wing of **Respecting Ourselves** is missing.

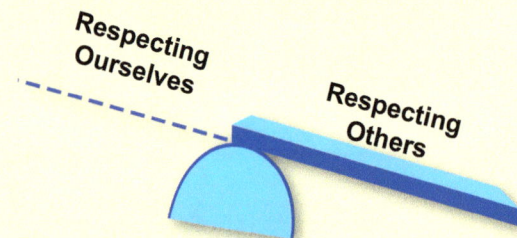

Respecting Ourselves

Respecting Others

"I mess up every time I try to do something. I am worthless."

Egotistic

The wing of **Respecting Others** is missing.

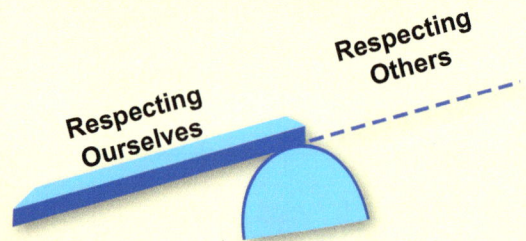

Respecting Ourselves

Respecting Others

"He is a moron. I am much better than he is."

22

It is natural to admire ourselves less on some days and more on other days. This variation is normal.

I got a bad grade today. I am the worst.

I got an award today. I am the best!

However, when we begin to hurt ourselves by continually feeling worthless, or start to hurt others by putting them down, it becomes a problem because we develop unbalanced thoughts.

Our **thoughts are balanced** when we respect ourselves and we respect others.

Balanced Thoughts

I am worthy and others are worthy too.

I am happy with what I have and happy with what others have too.

I want to progress and want others to progress too.

I appreciate myself and others.

Respecting Ourselves

Respecting Others

23

Having high self-esteem is essential for balancing our thoughts; respecting ourselves is in our control.

We develop high self-esteem when we respect ourselves:

1. We are satisfied with what we have today: our possessions, our health, and our relationships. Being content makes us happy, but it does not change our determination to work hard to improve in the future.

2. We appreciate our good qualities and achievements. Our abilities are different from others. Similarly, others will have talents that we don't have. Instead of feeling sad or envious, we should simply enjoy the talents of others while feeling proud of our own abilities.

3 We are proud of our heritage and ourselves. We should accept what cannot be changed and feel grateful for whoever we are. Every culture and heritage has its unique strengths, and there is something to learn from everyone.

I am proud of myself. I like the way I look. I like my heritage. I like my culture. I also like those who look different and have a different heritage. Hence, I learn from my culture and from other cultures.

4. We understand that making mistakes is a natural process. We should not expect to be proficient in everything without making mistakes. Instead, we should embrace our mistakes and look at them as opportunities to learn and improve.

5. We realize that we all have weaknesses. It is also necessary to recognize our strengths.

Our strengths and weaknesses are different from the strengths and weaknesses of others. There is a purpose for this variation: it gives us an opportunity to build relationships and grow.

If we have more, we help someone; if we have less, we ask for help.

It is also important to realize that there are so many skills that we cannot become perfect at everything. Some of our skills can be easily tested and measured such as math, science, and reasoning. Some skills are related to our values, habits, and behaviors such as motivation, kindness, teamwork, self-control, and honesty; these skills are difficult to measure. We are unique because we have different strengths and many of our good qualities cannot be measured. Therefore, we cannot and should not compare ourselves to anyone else.

If we compare one characteristic of our personality to that of someone else's, we may feel envious. Being envious is a normal emotion. However, if this feeling becomes persistent, then it is wrong because we may begin to …

Hurt ourselves:

- We develop low self-esteem.
- We stop enjoying life because we are constantly working to prove our superiority.

Hurt others:

- We gossip or spread rumors about them.
- We cheat or lie as we attempt to prove that we are better.

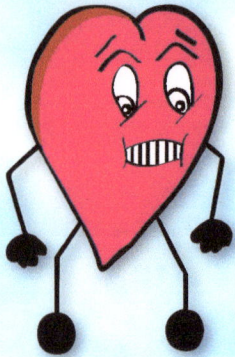

"She is a better singer. I am envious."

"She is popular. I am going to spread rumors about her and make myself more popular."

"He makes friends easily. I hate myself because I am so shy."

When we begin to feel envious, then it is time for us to reflect on our good qualities and think positively about ourselves. In the present moment, we should be grateful for and satisfied with our good qualities and achievements without comparing ourselves to others. For the future, we should continue to set goals for our advancement.

Sometimes we develop low self-esteem when others put us down or hurt us. Thinking good about ourselves and developing a culture of respect is in our hands. Therefore, we should respect ourselves and get motivated to increase awareness about mutual respect in our environment.

Respecting others is another factor essential for balancing our thoughts; it is in our control.

Just as we are worthy, others are worthy.
Just like we are not perfect, others are not perfect.
Just as we want to progress, others want to progress.
Just like we want to be helped, others want to be helped.

When we respect others, then …

• We embrace diversity and like others in spite of differences.

• We do not get tempted to hurt others by discriminating, harassing, lying, spreading rumors, or cheating.

• We do not gossip or put others down. If others are different or have a weakness, then we accept them the way they are or help them improve. If they make a mistake, then we correct their mistake either by communicating directly or with the help of a mediator, or by informing someone in authority. Helping others improve or helping others correct their mistakes is also respecting them. Gossiping or putting others down does no good because we are neither helping others improve nor helping them correct any mistakes.

27

With **balanced thoughts**, we are respectful of others, and we are happy with who we are and at peace with what we have. We are content.

What I have is different from what you have. I am happy for myself and for you. I am not envious.

Having balanced thoughts can help us differentiate between right and wrong actions.

Our thoughts will become unbalanced prior to any intentional wrong action.

Contentment is the blissful calmness of mind that we obtain when we have balanced thoughts in the present moment.

Contentment is not about the past or the future. It is about the present moment.

Past	This moment	Future

I was always the best singer in my school, but last year a new student got the best singer award. I was sad.

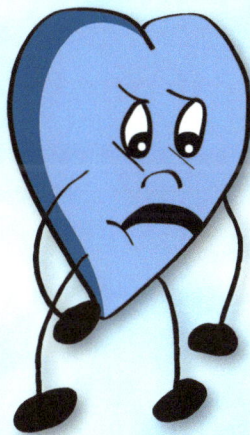

I am glad that I have the ability to work hard.

I am happy that I have been gifted with a good voice.

My goal is to work hard and get better at singing.

I will practice every day and compete again next year.

Past cannot be changed

Content

Future can be made

Contentment is in gaining wisdom from the past and accepting that history cannot be changed. By using the knowledge gained from our past experiences, we can set goals now to create a happy future.

CHAPTER 4 – ATTAINING CONTENTMENT

Just like we sleep to relax our body, we need to attain contentment to relax our mind. Then, we can work hard to progress. Contentment helps us enjoy the present moment and plan our future with a calm mind.

PROGRESS
↑
CONTENTMENT
↑
PROGRESS
↑
CONTENTMENT

Two Components for Attaining Contentment:

Balanced Thoughts

We are respectful of others and ourselves. We are satisfied with and grateful for everything we have.

Appreciation of the Present

We are not disturbed by events of the past or worried about the uncertainties of the future.

Learning to like the present moment is essential for attaining contentment. At times, however, we cannot enjoy the present moment because of disturbing thoughts about the past or the future.

Handling the Events of Our Past

No one's past is perfect. Everyone faces happy and sad times, pleasant and unpleasant occasions, fair and unfair moments. We should accept our past and understand that the past cannot be changed.

Positive experiences give us pleasant memories.
Remembering those happy moments and being grateful for everything we have will make us happy today.

"I participated in a singing event. I am so thankful that I have a good voice."

Negative experiences teach us something.
By gaining wisdom and learning from our past experiences, we can plan our future with a new vision.

"I lost my arm in an accident caused by someone who was texting and driving. Now I am educating everyone in my school district about this social issue. It is helping me accept my past and be happy."

Handling the Worries of Our Future

When we have the wisdom to accept what cannot be changed, and when we develop honest relationships, courage, the ability to work hard, and the strength not to give up, we can overcome our fear of failure and the worries about the future.

Methods to Relieve Worry and Attain Contentment

When our mind is disturbed, certain practices can help us keep our focus away from the past or worries about the future. These practices relax our mind and help us appreciate what we have.

1. Submitting to and praising God

and/or

2. Meditating and doing breathing exercises

"Give me the strength to accept what cannot be changed."

"Give me the knowledge to differentiate between right and wrong."

"Give me the ability to work hard and the patience to get the result that I expect."

"Give me the courage to stand for and do what is right."

"Give me the calmness to enjoy the present moment."

"Bless me and keep me safe."

"Make me humble, compassionate, and respectful of others."

"Help me to appreciate and be grateful for everything that I have."

and/or

3. Engrossing ourselves in activities that make us happy

Playing music, reading, writing, painting, exercising, taking care of animals or plants, enjoying nature, or doing any work honestly, happily, and diligently, without expecting anything in return, helps us attain the blissful calmness of mind we need to follow our dreams with happiness.

CHAPTER 5 – FOLLOWING OUR DREAMS

Two actions are needed to follow our dreams.

Action One - Attain Contentment

Contentment is the blissful calmness of mind that we obtain when we are satisfied with and grateful for who we are and what we have with us at the present moment without letting our mind get disturbed by the past or future. We achieve this peace of mind by respecting others and ourselves.

My journey to progress in life begins by improving my self-esteem. I realize that I am good even though I am not perfect; I look different, have weaknesses and strengths, and make mistakes like everyone else. My weaknesses, strengths, and mistakes give me opportunities to progress and build strong relationships with my family, friends, and teachers.

My high self-esteem also helps me to respect others. I realize that others also have weaknesses and strengths and I accept them the way they are. Others are different than I am but are also good. I help and support them whenever they need help. Through this process, I build strong relationships and begin to enjoy life.

Respectful environments and strong relationships make us courageous and help us overcome fears that can inhibit us from taking actions.

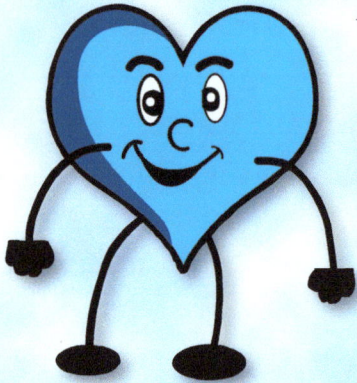

I have supporting family and friends. I know if I get hurt, they will be there to help me. They consider me worthy even if I make a mistake or am unable to do something. In fact, they not only appreciate my good qualities, but also help me improve my habits and abilities. This support gives me the confidence to make an effort. I do not fear making a mistake or facing an apparent failure.

Just like they support me, I support them when they are in need. I never put them down or laugh at their mistakes or weaknesses. Instead, I help them improve.

We disagree and argue over several issues, but we never gossip about or criticize each other in public; we never doubt our love and support for each other. This strong bond between us has given us the confidence that we are never alone; we are here for each other in good and bad times.

Taking time to relax, enjoy, and be grateful for everything we have is also essential to attaining contentment. Enjoying fun activities while having balanced thoughts, without worrying about the past or future, and without expecting anything in return, is pure happiness.

34

Action Two - Progress

Life becomes boring if we stop progressing. Also, we can start to have negative thoughts when we are not thinking about something constructive. Therefore, it is imperative to be inquisitive and keep improving.

How do we progress?

A - Set Correct Goals

Each one of us is an individual, a member of various groups, and a part of society. Therefore, there are many ways to progress in our lives. Correct goals are for …

1. Self-improvement.

2. Advancement of our family and the groups with whom we work.

3. Betterment of society: because we are a part of society, improvement of our society is also our progress.

I want to be rich and popular. That is why I want to become a singer.

I feel happy when I sing. It is my passion. I practice singing every day.

If money, awards, power, and popularity are made as primary goals, then they can tempt us to hurt others.

B - Be Realistic

1. We should accept that our past and our heritage cannot be changed.

2. We should understand that we cannot be perfect in everything.

3. We should realize that we will not get the result that we expect all the time.

C - Learn To Focus

To focus means to pay attention only to the task that we are doing: we are thinking about the work we are physically doing, and our mind is not wandering. Our thoughts and our actions are synchronized.

I put my phone away when I am working on my project. Then, my thoughts are centered on my project; my mind is not distracted. When I take a break, I will focus on socializing and communicating with my friends.

D - Be Honest

When we are honest, we become courageous because honesty removes the fear of being caught or punished.

E - Be Flexible and Aware of the Changing Conditions

As we progress, the conditions may vary. Being flexible means that we are open-minded, able to learn new ways, and willing to change the plan after analyzing the new situation. Therefore, we should stay aware of the changing conditions, think about the options, and modify the plan if needed.

The auditorium is not available for practice today. Some people are working on repairs. We will practice in a different room even though that place is not perfect.

WE NEED TO PRACTICE IN THE AUDITORIUM! I AM GOING TO TELL EVERYONE TO STOP REPAIRS AND LET US PRACTICE.

Sometimes, we should stand firm; we should not cheat or hurt others or ourselves in any situation. No one should be able to force us to do anything wrong.

For the fundraiser, everyone has already pre-paid for the cookies. Now we don't have to worry about the quality. We can work fast and finish our job.

NO! NO! We must put in our time and effort to make the best cookies. We will not cheat anyone.

It is important, therefore, to be aware of the situation and assess whether to be flexible or to stay firm.

F - Build Relationships and Help Each Other Improve

Just like we should be adaptable to a situation, we should be flexible regarding our opinions of other people. People make mistakes, but they also improve. Sometimes, we fail to notice the strengths of other people. Being rigid and not accepting those who have made a mistake in the past, or not accepting others because they are different, is wrong. We lose on building relationships and progressing in life.

He lied to me in the past. Even though he truly apologized, I am never going to like him again.

STOP

THIS IS BEING RIGID.

She was addicted to drugs. She went through rehabilitation and seems to be doing fine, but I will never talk to her.

He can never improve.

Some people correct their behaviors, and some people begin to hurt others. Therefore, it is important to be aware of the changing behaviors and take appropriate actions.

When someone truly apologizes and corrects his or her behavior, accepting the apology and moving forward is our greatness.

If someone is intentionally hurting others, correcting his or her behavior is essential. In such situations, we may need the help of someone in authority.

G - Learn From Mistakes

Just like children cannot learn to walk without falling, we cannot progress in our lives without making mistakes; this is a natural process. Therefore, we should not fear making mistakes. Accepting our mistakes requires courage; it helps us take responsibility and motivates us to work harder and improve our skills. Denying our mistakes or blaming others for them is wrong; it makes us weak and fearful and prevents us from progressing happily in life.

We become wiser when we learn from every mistake we make. Parents, teachers, and friends who help us correct our mistakes are our well-wishers because they are helping us to progress in our lives.

H - Overcome Obstacles

We should know our weaknesses and …

- **Work hard** to improve our skills.
- **Accept help and advice** from others and be thankful for their support.
- **Form strong teams** by respecting each other, handling disagreements by communicating clearly and honestly, listening to everyone's opinion, and choosing the best option.

I - Understand Failure and Success

If we work very hard and do not get the result that we expect, then it is not a true failure. Using the wisdom gained from our experiences, we can modify our plans to set up goals for the future.

True success is an ongoing progress. We always progress when we work hard. Therefore, as long as we are not giving up, we are always on the path to success.

True failure is not making an effort or is giving up.

Examples of Failure

"I fear I will be rejected.
Therefore, I am not going to try."

"I fear people will laugh at me.
Therefore, I am not going to try."

"I got poor grades in my junior year.
Therefore, I quit school."

TRY, TRY, AND TRY AGAIN WITHOUT GIVING UP!

We always progress, gain experience, and learn something every time we try. This ongoing progress is our success. No matter what the result is, there is wisdom and happiness on our journey to challenge ourselves and improve.

J - Be Courageous and Face Fears Head-On

It is important to know the risks and then have the courage to face them. If there is an adverse outcome, we should accept it and not get discouraged; we should not give up.

"I know I can get rejected, yet I will try."

"I know I may not get a good result, yet I will try."

"I have the courage to go out of my comfort zone and try something that I wouldn't try earlier."

We need courage to

Protect everyone's rights and stand for equality and respect:

We must fight against our temptations to lie, cheat, hate, or hurt others.

We must stand against those who are treating others with disrespect.

Improve our relationships and skills:

There is no fear of being lonely or being laughed at when we work to create respectful environments.

There is no fear of failure when we are determined not to give up.

Learning how to progress helps us develop **grit**: the quality of advancing in life without giving up.

Sometimes, on our journey to progress, we fall down and get hurt. We experience a setback and lose our possessions or get hurt physically, emotionally, or socially. Accepting what has happened, attaining contentment, and then setting up a goal for self-improvement on this new path will make us happy again. This quality of recovering from a setback and restarting the journey to progress is **resilience**.

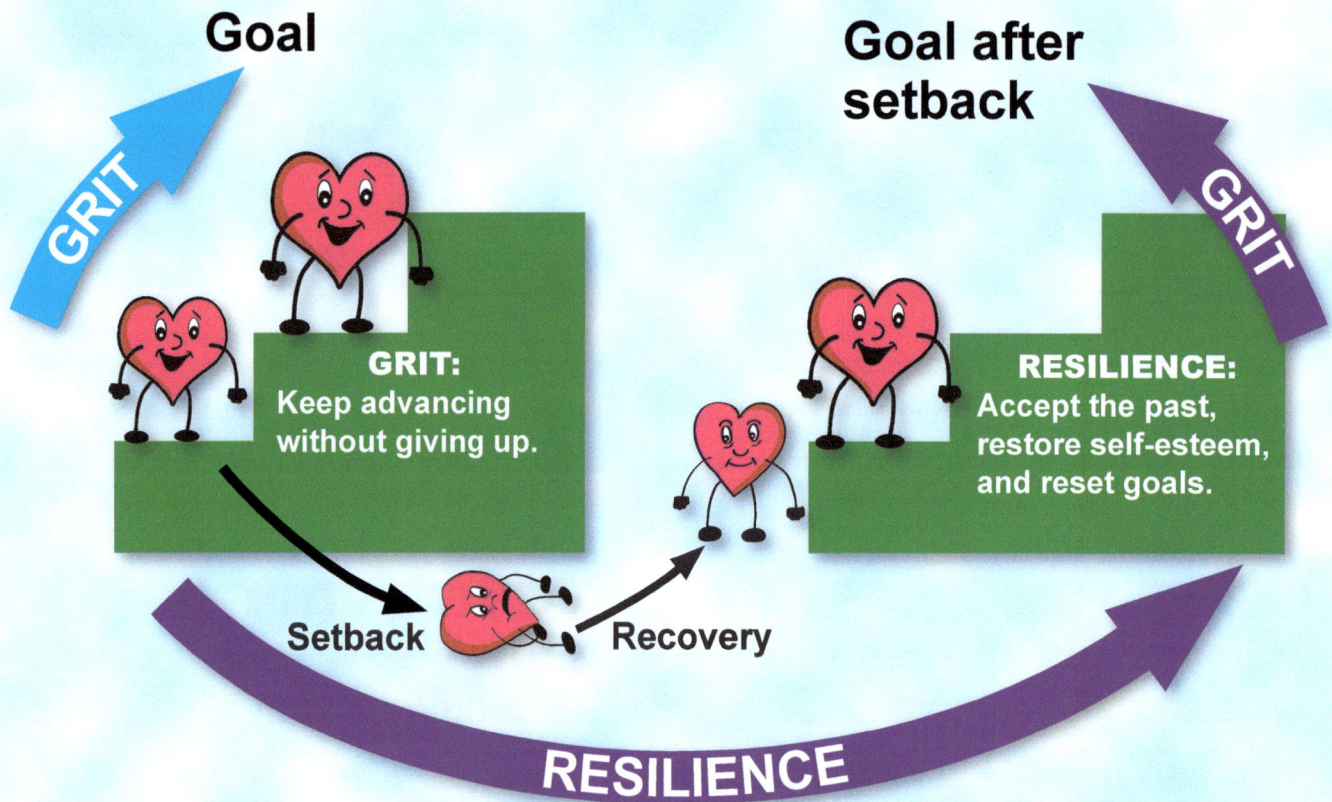

Goal

GRIT

Goal after setback

GRIT

GRIT:
Keep advancing without giving up.

RESILIENCE:
Accept the past, restore self-esteem, and reset goals.

Setback **Recovery**

RESILIENCE

Resilience + Grit = Following our Dreams

Healthy relationships are buffers that support us during difficult times; they give us emotional comfort, assist us to overcome our weaknesses, correct our mistakes, and help us become courageous to progress in life.

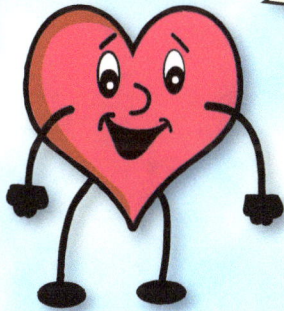

We are happy and enjoying life because …

1. We have a strong relationship; we are there for each other in good and bad times.

2. We are progressing in life.

3. We are grateful for and satisfied with what we have at this moment. We are content today and desire to keep progressing in the future. Our contentment helps us enjoy the present and helps us plan our future with a calm mind.

The purpose of our life is to progress happily by respecting others and ourselves; this is the legacy that we follow and leave behind.

Therefore, we all should have goals and build healthy relationships. Then, each one of us can say with confidence,

"I CAN FACE MY FEARS TO FOLLOW MY DREAMS."

Developing a culture of respect and changing the social environment is essential.

The simple language and format of this book can help develop a thorough understanding for all adults. Parents and teachers can then educate and discuss with children about the complex subject of progressing happily in life.

www.ingramcontent.com/pod-product-compliance
Lightning Source LLC
LaVergne TN
LVHW072125070426

835511LV00003B/88